A Note to Parents

DK READERS is a compelling program for beginning readers, designed in conjunction with leading literacy experts, including Dr. Linda Gambrell, Distinguished Professor of Education at Clemson University. Dr. Gambrell has served as President of the National Reading Conference, the College Reading Association, and the International Reading Association.

Beautiful illustrations and superb full-color photographs combine with engaging, easy-to-read stories to offer a fresh approach to each subject in the series. Each DK READER is guaranteed to capture a child's interest while developing his or her reading skills, general knowledge, and love of reading.

The five levels of DK READERS are aimed at different reading abilities, enabling you to choose the books that are exactly right for your child:

Pre-level 1: Learning to read
Level 1: Beginning to read
Level 2: Beginning to read alone
Level 3: Reading alone
Level 4: Proficient readers

The "normal" age at which a child begins to read can be anywhere from three to eight years old. Adult participation through the lower levels is very helpful for providing encouragement, discussing storylines, and sounding out unfamiliar words.

No matter which level you select, you can be sure that you are helping your child learn to read, then read to learn!

LONDON, NEW YORK, MUNICH,
MELBOURNE, and DELHI

DK LONDON
Series Editor Deborah Lock
US Senior Editor Shannon Beatty
Project Art Editor Hoa Luc
Producers, Pre-production
Francesca Wardell, Vikki Nousiainen
Illustrator Tim McDonagh

Reading Consultant
Linda Gambrell, Ph.D.

DK DELHI
Editor Nandini Gupta
Assistant Art Editor Yamini Panwar
DTP Designers Anita Yadav, Mohammad Usman
Picture Researcher Deepak Negi
Deputy Managing Editor Soma B. Chowdhury

First American Edition, 2014
Published in the United States by DK Publishing
345 Hudson Street, New York, New York 10014

14 15 16 17 18 10 9 8 7 6 5 4 3 2 1
001—256577—June/14

A catalog record for this book is available
from the Library of Congress.

ISBN: 978-1-4654-1997-2 (Paperback)
ISBN: 978-1-4654-1996-5 (Hardcover)

DK books are available at special discounts when
purchased in bulk for sales promotions, premiums,
fund-raising, or educational use.
For details, contact:
DK Publishing Special Markets
345 Hudson Street, New York, New York 10014
SpecialSales@dk.com

Printed and bound in China by
South China Printing Company

The publisher would like to thank the following for
their kind permission to reproduce their photographs:
(Key: a=above, b=below/bottom, c=center, l=left, r=right, t=top)
32 Dorling Kindersley: Laszlo Veres (tl, cr, clb).
Jacket images: Front cover: Corbis: age fotostock Spain S.L. /
Fco. Javier Gutiérrez

All other images © Dorling Kindersley Limited
For further information see: www.dkimages.com

Discover more at
www.dk.com

DK READERS

BEGINNING

1

TO READ

Little Dolphin

Written by Sue Unstead

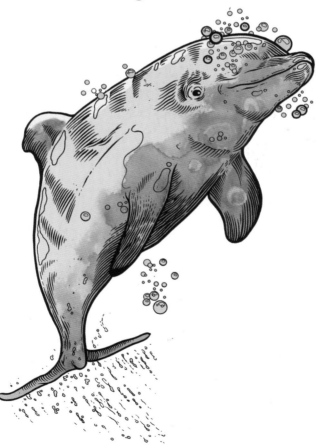

Little Dolphin lives
in the sparkly blue sea.
As soon as he was born,
his mama took him
up, up, up to snatch
his very first breath
of air.

Mama calls to Little Dolphin
all the time.
"Wheee, wheee!
Where are you?"

Little Dolphin calls back to her.
He has his own song,
"Wheee, whooooa!
Here I am, Mama."

Little Dolphin stays close
to his mama.
She teaches him how to dive
and how to leap over
the waves.
But he longs to play with
the bigger dolphins.

"When can I join them?"
he asks.
"When you can swim fast,
Little Dolphin," says Mama.

Little Dolphin grows bigger
every day.
"I can swim fast.
I can leap and dive," he says.
Mama says, "Now you are
ready for Dolphin School.
Remember to stay
with the other dolphins.
Watch the leader.
Look out for big boats."

Little Dolphin swims away
with a swish of his tail.
He joins the other dolphins.
They play follow-the-leader.
They play catch-that-fish.
They see who can jump
the highest.
"Wheee, wheeoa."
"Click-click-click."

Rrrr, rumble, rumble, rrrr.

"Listen! What is that sound?" asks the biggest dolphin.

"A ship! It is a ship's engine,"
cries another dolphin.
"Quick! Let's chase it,"
says the biggest dolphin.

Here comes the ship!
A foamy wave pushes through
the water.
"Wheee!
Let's dive under it.
Whooah!
Let's jump in front of it,"
say the dolphins.

Splash! Splash!

"This is fun!" says Little Dolphin.

There is a dark shadow
above them.
Little Dolphin hears the thump
of the engine.
He feels the swoosh
from the propellers.
"Oooh! It is scary,"
thinks Little Dolphin.
He swims fast.

"Help! I cannot keep up,"
says Little Dolphin.
"The ship is too fast for me.
Where is everyone?
Click-click-click."

No one answers.
Little Dolphin is alone.
"Wheee, whoa, Maaama!"
he cries.

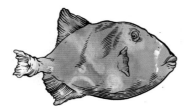

Whoosh!

Little Dolphin pops his head
out of the water.
"Look! There is a white sail.
It must be a boat.
I will follow you,"
thinks Little Dolphin.
A girl on board the boat
sees Little Dolphin.
The girl is called Rosie.

23

The fishing boat chugs back
to port.
Little Dolphin follows,
tired and lost.
"You must go back out
to sea," says Rosie.
She runs to fetch
her own small boat.
"I must save Little Dolphin,"
she thinks.

She remembers what her own
mama told her when she was
a young girl.
"Stay with the school,
watch the leader, and
look out for big boats,"
she thinks.

"Follow me, Little Dolphin,"
she calls.
Little Dolphin follows
her small boat.

Out in the bay, Little Dolphin
hears his mama calling,
"Wheee, whee!
Where are you?"
"Wheee, whooa!" he cries.
"Here I am, Mama!"

Rosie sees two dolphins leaping.
She thinks they are smiling, too.
What a happy day!

Dolphin Facts

Smart dolphins

Dolphins are clever animals and love to play.

Friendly dolphins

They live in groups of 10 to 12 dolphins called pods, or schools.

Long life

A dolphin can live for 25 years.

Hold your breath

A dolphin usually comes up to the surface for breath every two minutes, but can hold its breath for much longer.

Index

bay 28

boat 10, 22,
  24, 26, 27

breath 4

call 6, 7, 27, 28

dive 8, 10, 17

engine 15, 18

fish 12

jump 12, 17

leader 10,
  12, 26

leap 8, 10, 29

pod 30

port 24

propellers 18

school 10, 26

sea 4, 24

ship 15, 17, 20

swim 9, 10,
  12, 18

tail 12

DK READERS help children learn to read, then read to learn. If you enjoyed this DK READER, then look out for these other titles for your child.

Level 1 Deadly Dinosaurs
Roar! Thud! Meet Rexy, Sid, Deano, and Sonia, the dinosaurs that come alive at night in the museum. Who do you think is the deadliest?

Level 1 Playful Puppy
Holly's dream has come true—she's been given her very own puppy. Share her delight in the playfulness of her new puppy as she tries to train him.

Level 1 Bugs Hide and Seek
Surprise! Some bugs have the perfect shape and color to stay hidden. They look like the plants around them. Can you spot them?

Level 1 Mega Machines
Hard hats on! The mega machines are very busy building a new school. Watch them in action!

Level 1 Pirate Attack!
Come and join Captain Blackbeard and his pirate crew for an action-packed adventure on the high seas.